KNOCK KNOCK, WHO'S THERE? JOKES

KNOCK KNOCK, WHO'S THERE? JOKES

ARCTURUS

ARCTURUS

This edition published in 2013 by
Arcturus Publishing Limited
26/27 Bickels Yard, 151–153 Bermondsey Street,
London SE1 3HA

Written by Karen King
Illustrated by Peter Coupe
Edited by Becca Clunes

ISBN: 978-1-78212-391-0
CH003716EN
Supplier 03, Date 0413, Print run 2652

Printed in China

Knock, knock...

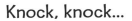

Who's there?

Adair.

Adair who?

Adair once
but I'm bald now!

Knock, knock...

Who's there?

Twitter.

Twitter who?

Have you got an owl in there?

Knock, knock...

Who's there?

Canoe.

Canoe who?

Canoe come out
and play today?

Knock, knock...

Who's there?

Geezer.

Geezer who?

Geezer couple of minutes
and I'll pick the lock.

Knock, knock...

Who's there?

Ellie.

Ellie who?

Ellie Funt.

Knock, knock...

Who's there?

Police.

Police who?

Police let me in, it's freezing
out here!

Knock, knock...

Who's there?

Stan.

Stan who?

Stan back, I'm breaking
the door down!

Knock, knock...

Who's there?

Anka.

Anka who?

Anka the ship!

Knock, knock...

Who's there?

Barbara.

Barbara who?

Barbara black sheep!

Knock, knock...

Who's there?

Amos.

Amos who?

Amosquito just bit me!

Knock, knock...

Who's there?

Atomic.

Atomic who?

Atomic ache.

Knock, knock...

Who's there?

Irish stew.

Irish stew who?

Irish stew in the name
of the law!

Knock, knock...

Who's there?

Andy.

Andy who?

Andy mosquito bit me again!

Knock, knock...

Who's there?

Granny.

Granny who?

Knock knock.

Who's there?

Granny.

Granny who?

Knock, knock.

Who's there?

Aunt.

Aunt who?

Aren't you glad that Granny's gone?

Knock, knock...

Who's there?

Doris.

Doris who?

Doris jammed that's why
I had to knock.

Knock, knock...

Who's there?

Eileen Dover.

Eileen Dover who?

Eileen Dover your fence
and broke it!

Knock, knock...

Who's there?

Affro.

Affro who?

Affro'd my ball into your garden.

Knock, knock...

Who's there?

Adolf.

Adolf who?

Adolf ball hid me in di moud
and I cand dalk prober dow.

Knock, knock...

Who's there?

A man.

A man who?

A man with a wooden leg.

Tell him to hop it!

Knock, knock...

Who's there?

Ally.

Ally who?

Allygator.

Knock, knock...

Who's there?

Aurora.

Aurora who?

Aurora just come
from a big lion!

Knock, knock...

Who's there?

Dana.

Dana who?

Dana talk with your mouth full.

Knock, knock...

Who's there?

Howell.

Howell who?

Howell you have your toast?
With marmalade or honey?

Knock, knock...

Who's there?

Sonia.

Sonia who?

Sonia shoe. I can smell it
from here.

Knock, knock...

Who's there?

Phil.

Phil who?

Phil this cup with sugar
would you,
I've just run out!

Knock, knock...

Who's there?

Munchin.

Munchin who?

Munchin my dinner and need a drink.

Knock, knock...

Who's there?

Paul.

Paul who?

Paul lady who's just fell in a puddle!

Knock, knock...

Who's there?

Cora.

Cora who?

Cora wish I had a front door
like this!

Knock, knock...

Who's there?

Tristan.

Tristan who?

Tristan an insect to get up
your nose!

Knock, knock...

Who's there?

Lucy.

Lucy who?

Lucy elastic can be
embarrassing!

Knock, knock...

Who's there?

Whoopi.

Whoopi who?

Whoopi cushion!

Knock, knock...

Who's there?

Island.

Island who?

Island on your roof with
my parachute!

Knock, knock...

Who's there?

Russell.

Russell who?

Russell be home
in a minute - put the kettle on!

Knock, knock...

Who's there?

Barry.

Barry who?

Barry the treasure then no one
will find it!

Knock, knock...

Who's there?

Tex.

Tex who?

Tex two to tango.

Knock, knock...

Who's there?

Donalette.

Donalette who?

Donalette the bed bugs bite!

Knock, knock...

Who's there?

Hali.

Hali who?

Halitosis - your breath smells yuk!

Knock, knock...

Who's there?

Zombie.

Zombie who?

Zombies make honey, others
are Queens!

Knock, knock...

Who's there?

Noah.

Noah who?

Noah good place to eat?

Knock, knock...

Who's there?

Abba.

Abba who?

Aba'out turn, Quick march!

Knock, knock...

Who's there?

Aida.

Aida who?

Aida whole village 'cos
I'm a monster!

Knock, knock...

Who's there?

Vera.

Vera who?

Vera long way from home
and need a map!

Knock, knock...

Who's there?

Lillian.

Lillian who?

Lillian the garden!

Knock, knock...

Who's there?

Aleta.

Aleta who?

Aleta from your head teacher!

Knock, knock...

Who's there?

Alf.

Alf who?

Alf all if you don't catch me!

Knock, knock...

Who's there?

Althea.

Althea who?

Althea in court!

Knock, knock...

Who's there?

Paul.

Paul who?

Paul the other one
it's got bells on!

Knock, knock...

Who's there?

Alison.

Alison who?

Alison at the keyhole
sometimes...

Knock, knock...

Who's there?

Argo.

Argo who?

Argo to piano lessons
after school!

Knock, knock...

Who's there?

Army.

Army who?

Army aunts coming for tea?

Knock, knock...

Who's there?

Betty.

Betty who?

Betty earns a lot of money!

Knock, knock...

Who's there?

Thumping.

Thumping who?

Thumping green and slimy
is crawling up your back!

Knock, knock...

Who's there?

Double Glazing Salesman.

...

... hello...? hello...?

Knock, knock...

Who's there?

Twyla.

Twyla who?

Twilight is when the vampires come out!

Knock, knock...

Who's there?

Glasgow.

Glasgow who?

Glasgow get out of here, it's creepy!

Knock, knock...

Who's there?

Augusta.

Augusta who?

Augusta wind blew my house away!!

Knock, knock...

Who's there?

Benin.

Benin who?

Benin in hell. It was awful!

Knock, knock...

Who's there?

Auntie.

Auntie who?

Auntie glad to see me again!

Knock, knock...

Who's there?

Baby Owl.

Baby Owl who?

Baby Owl see you
later, baby not!

Knock, knock...

Who's there?

Chester.

Chester who?

Chester drawers!

Knock, knock...

Who's there?

Harmony.

Harmony who?

Harmony times do I have
to tell you?!

SIGH...

Knock, knock...

Who's there?

Bacon.

Bacon who?

Bacon a cake in the oven!

Knock, knock...

Who's there?

Sadie.

Sadie who?

Sadie magic word and
watch me disappear!

Knock, knock...

Who's there?

Ben Hur.

Ben Hur who?

Ben Hur an hour - let me in!

Knock, knock...

Who's there?

Cliff.

Cliff who?

Cliff hanger!

Knock, knock...

Who's there?

Bea.

Bea who?

Bea love and open the door.

Knock, knock...

Who's there?

Bean.

Bean who?

Bean anywhere nice
on your holidays?

Knock, knock...

Who's there?

Viper.

Viper who?

Viper nose, it keeps running!

Knock, knock...

Who's there?

Dishes.

Dishes who?

Dishes a nice place!

Knock, knock...

Who's there?

Bertha.

Bertha who?

Berthaday girl!

Knock, knock...

Who's there?

Chopin.

Chopin who?

Chopin the supermarket.

Knock, knock...

Who's there?

Don.

Don who?

Don be afraid...
look into my
eyes...
you are feeling
sleepy...

Knock, knock...

Who's there?

Jess.

Jess who?

Jess me and my
shadow!

Knock, knock...

Who's there?

Caesar.

Caesar who?

Caesar jolly good fellow.

Knock, knock...

Who's there?

Oink, oink.

Oink, oink who?

Make up your mind are you
a pig or an owl!

Knock, knock...

Who's there?

Duck.

Duck who?

Just duck - they're throwing
things at us!

Knock, knock...

Who's there?

Kari.

Kari who?

Kari on like this and I'll freeze
to death out here!

Knock, knock...

Who's there?

Carlo.

Carlo who?

Carload of junk!

Knock, knock...

Who's there?

Carmen.

Carmen who?

Carmen like best is a Ferrari!

Knock, knock...

Who's there?

Spider.

Spider who?

Spider what everyone says,
I like you!

Knock, knock...

Who's there?

Cello.

Cello who?

Cello, how are you?

Knock, knock...

Who's there?

Muffin.

Muffin who?

Muffin the matter with me.
How about you?

Knock, knock...

Who's there?

Aries.

Aries who?

Aries a reason I'm knocking
at your door!

Knock, knock...

Who's there?

Ben.

Ben who?

Ben down and tie
your shoelaces!

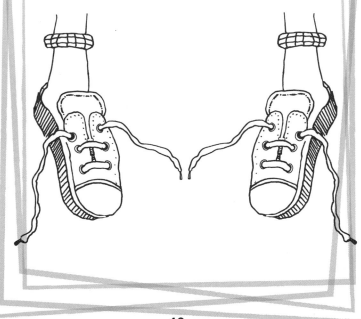

Knock, knock...

Who's there?

A ghost.

A ghost who?

Thought it would scare you!

Knock, knock...

Who's there?

Guthrie.

Guthrie who?

Guthrie blind mice!

Knock, knock...

Who's there?

Congo.

Congo who?

Congo into the woods, it's dangerous!

Knock, knock...

Who's there?

Tom.

Tom Sawyer who?

Tom Sawyer underwear!

Knock, knock...

Who's there?

Diesel.

Diesel who?

Diesel make you feel better!

Knock, knock...

Who's there?

Devlin.

Devlin who?

Devlin a red dress!

Knock, knock...

Who's there?

Soup.

Soup who?

Souperman!

Knock, knock...

Who's there?

Dwayne.

Dwayne who?

Dwayne the bathtub,
it's overflowing!

Knock, knock...

Who's there?

Ahab.

Ahab who?

Ahab to go to the toilet.
Quick, open the door!

Knock, knock...

Who's there?

Derek.

Derek who?

Derek get richer and the poor get poorer!

Knock, knock...

Who's there?

Snow.

Snow who?

Snow use I've lost my key again!

Knock, knock...

Who's there?

Drum.

Drum who?

Drum as fast as you can!

Knock, knock...
Who's there?
Salmon.
Salmon who?
Salmon-chanted evening!

Knock, knock...
Who's there?
Dublin.
Dublin who?
Dublin up with laughter!

Knock, knock...
Who's there?
Yvette.
Yvette who?
Yvette helps lots of animals.

Knock, knock...

Who's there?

Ivor.

Ivor who?

Ivor saw hand from knocking!

Knock, knock...

Who's there?

CD's.

CD's who?

CD's fingers?
They're freezing - let me in!

Knock, knock...

Who's there?

Rhoda.

Rhoda who?

Row, Row, Rhoda boat!

Knock, knock...

Who's there?

Turner.

Turner who?

Turner round there's a monster
behind you!

Knock, knock...

Who's there?

Rita.

Rita who?

Rita novel!

Knock, knock...

Who's there?

Kent.

Kent who?

Kent you tell by my voice?

Knock, knock...

Who's there?

Toffee.

Toffee who?

Toffee loved is the best feeling
in the world!

Knock, knock...

Who's there?

Tuna.

Tuna who?

Tuna whole orchestra!

Knock, knock...

Who's there ?

Henrietta.

Henrietta who ?

Henrietta worm that was
in his apple !

Knock, knock...

Who's there?

Sarah.

Sarah who?

Sarah phone I can use?

Knock, knock...

Who's there?

Olive.

Olive who?

Olive right next door to you!

Knock, knock...

Who's there?

Wooden shoe.

Wooden shoe who?

Wooden shoe like to hear
another joke?

Knock, knock...

Who's there?

Ivan.

Ivan who?

Ivan idea you will know as soon
as you open the door!

Knock, knock...

Who's there?

Amanda.

Amanda who?

Amanda the table!

Knock, knock...

Who's there?

Turkey.

Turkey who?

Turkey and find out!

Knock, knock...

Who's there?

Champ.

Champ who?

Champ poo your hair it's dirty!

Knock, knock...

Who's there?

Eugene.

Eugene who?

Eugene, me Tarzan !

Knock, knock...

Who's there?

Topic.

Topic who?

Topic a wild flower
is against the law.

Knock, knock...

Who's there?

Grey.

Grey who?

Greyt balls of fire!

Knock, knock...

Who's there?

Cheese.

Cheese who?

Cheese a cute girl.

Knock, knock...

Who's there?

Willy.

Willy who?

Willy lend me a street map,
I'm a stranger in town!

Knock, knock...

Who's there?

Wade.

Wade who?

Wade down upon
the Swanee River!

Knock, Knock...

Who's there?

Shelby.

Shelby who?

Shelby coming round the
mountain when she comes!

Knock, knock...

Who's there?

Steve.

Steve who?

Steve upper lip!

Knock, knock...

Who's there?

Rufus.

Rufus who?

Rufus on fire!

Knock, knock...

Who's there?

Cattle.

Cattle who?

Cattle purr if you stroke it!

Knock, knock...

Who's there?

Mary Lee.

Mary Lee who?

Mary Lee, Mary Lee, life is just a dream. Row, row...

Knock, knock...

Who's there?

Isadore.

Isadore who?

Isadore on the right way round?

Knock, knock...

Who's there?

Patty O

Patty O who?

Patty O furniture!

Knock, knock...

Who's there?

Butcher.

Butcher who?

Butcher left leg in,
your left leg out...

Knock, knock...

Who's there?

Carol.

Carol who?

Carol go if you switch
the ignition on!

Knock, knock...

Who's there?

Dakota.

Dakota who?

Dakota is too small!

Knock, knock...

Who's there?

Paul.

Paul who?

Paul the door open a bit,
my coat is trapped!

Knock, knock...

Who's there?

Edwin.

Edwin who?

Edwin a cup if he could
run faster!

Knock, knock...

Who's there?

Gopher.

Gopher who?

Gopher help, I'm stuck in the mud!

Knock, knock...

Who's there?

Esau.

Esau who?

Esau you in the bath!

Knock, knock...

Who's there?

Abba, Abba.

Abba, Abba Who?

Abba Merry Christmas and
Abba Happy New Year!

Knock, knock...

Who's there?

Cecile.

Cecile who?

Cecile th-the windows. Th-there's a m-monster out there.

Knock, knock...

Who's there?

Butch.

Butch who?

Butch your little arms around me!

Knock, knock...

Who's there?

Howl.

Howl who?

Howl you know unless you open the door!

Knock, Knock!

Who's there?

Vidor.

Vidor who?

Vidor better open soon...!

Knock, knock...

Who's there?

Witches.

Witches who?

Witches the way to go home?

Knock, knock...

Who's there?

Leena.

Leena who?

Leena a little closer and
I'll whisper in your ear!

Knock, knock...

Who's there?

Señor!

Señor who?

Señor underpants!

Knock, knock...

Who's there?

Daisy.

Daisy who?

Daisy that you are out but
I don't believe them!

Knock, knock...

Who's there?

Mara.

Mara who?

Mara, Mara on the wall!

Knock, knock...

Who's there?

Olivia.

Olivia who?

Olivia, so get out of my house!

Knock, knock...

Who's there?

Gorilla.

Gorilla who?

Gorilla cheese sandwich for me
and I'll be right over!

Knock, knock...

Who's there?

Ashley.

Ashley who?

Bless you!

Knock, knock...

Who's there?

Cole.

Cole who?

Cole as a cucumber!

Knock, knock...

Who's there?

Veal chop.

Veal chop who?

Veal chop around and see if we
can pick up some bargains!

Knock, knock...

Who's there?

Eames.

Eames who?

Eames to please!

Knock, knock...

Who's there?

Teddy.

Teddy who?

Teddy is the beginning of the
rest of your life!

Knock, knock...

Who's there?

Winnie Thup.

Winnie Thup who?

And Tigger came too!

Knock, knock...

Who's there?

Thayer.

Thayer who?

Thayer thorry or I'll throw thith
pie in your face!

Knock, knock...

Who's there?

Utica.

Utica who?

Utica the high road and
I'll taka the low road!

Knock, knock...

Who's there?

Diana.

Diana who?

Diana of thirst, can I have a glass of water please?

Knock, knock...

Who's there?

Freda.

Freda who?

Freda jolly good fellow!

Knock, knock...

Who's there?

Telly.

Telly who?

Telly your friend to come out!

Knock, knock...

Who's there?

Ethan.

Ethan who?

Ethan too much makes you fat!

Knock, knock...

Who's there?

Actor.

Actor who?

Actor you, my dear!

Knock, knock...

Who's there?

Harry.

Harry who?

Harry up!
There's a monster after us!

Knock, knock...

Who's there?

Ear.

Ear who?

Ear you are - a letter.

Knock, knock...
Who's there?
Yah.
Yah who?
Yahoo! Ride'em, cowboy!

Knock, knock...
Who's there?
Fergie.
Fergie who?
Fergiedness sake let me in!

Knock, knock...
Who's there?
Ears.
Ears who?
Ears some more jokes for you!

Knock, knock...

Who's there?

Scott.

Scott who?

Scott a creepy look about it,
this place. I think it's haunted!

Knock, knock...

Who's there?

Fangs.

Fangs who?

Fangs for the memory!

Knock, knock...

Who's there?

Rhino.

Rhino who?

Rhino every joke there is!

Knock, knock...

Who's there?

Edward.

Edward who?

Edward like to play now please!

Knock, knock...

Who's there?

Farrah.

Farrah who?

Farrah'nough!

Knock, knock...

Who's there?

Ida.

Ida who?

Ida know why I love you like I do!

Knock, knock...

Who's there?

Keith.

Keith who?

Keith your hands off me!

Knock, knock...

Who's there?

Wayne.

Wayne who?

Wayne in a manger!

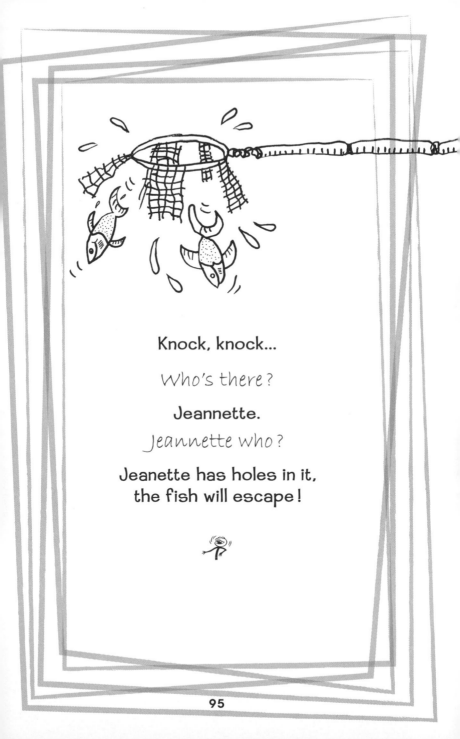

Knock, knock...

Who's there?

Jeannette.

Jeannette who?

Jeanette has holes in it, the fish will escape!

Knock, knock...

Who's there?

Ivan.

Ivan who?

Ivan infectious disease!

Knock, knock...

Who's there?

Venice.

Venice who?

Venice this door going to open?

Knock, knock...

Who's there?

Acid.

Acid who?

Acid down and be quiet!

Knock, knock...

Who's there?

Honey bee.

Honey bee who?

Honey bee a sweetie
and let me in!

Knock, knock...

Who's there?

Diego.

Diego who?

Diego before de 'B'.

Knock, knock...

Who's there?

Yolanda.

Yolanda who?

Yolanda some money!

Knock, knock...

Who's there?

Duane.

Duane who?

Duane gonna get away with dis!

Knock, knock...

Who's there?

Sara.

Sara who?

Sara man delivering milk here yesterday - do you think he could deliver some to me too?

Knock, knock...

Who's there?

Illegal.

Illegal who?

**Illegal stays in the nest until
it feels better!**

Knock, knock...

Who's there?

Major.

Major who?

Major headache, can you get
me an aspirin?

Knock, knock...

Who's there?

Dozen.

Dozen who?

Dozen anyone know my name?

Knock, knock...

Who's there?

Candy.

Candy who?

Candy cow jump over de moon?

Knock, knock...

Who's there?

Norm.

Norm who?

**Norm more Mr Nice Guy –
OPEN
THIS DOOR !**

Knock, knock...

Who's there?

Gary.

Gary who?

Gary on smiling!

Knock, knock...

Who's there?

Hannah.

Hannah who?

Hannah Happy New Year!

Knock, knock...

Who's there?

Ghandi.

Ghandi who?

Ghandi come out to play?

Knock, knock...

Who's there?

Julie.

Julie who?

Julie your door unlocked?

Knock, knock...

Who's there?

Zizi.

Zizi who?

Zizi when you know how!

Knock, knock...

Who's there?

Fork.

Fork who?

Forket him - he isn't worth it!

Knock, knock...

Who's there?

Amanda.

Amanda who?

Amanda fix the boiler.

Knock, knock...

Who's there?

Phyllis.

Phyllis who?

Phyllis bucket with water, please.

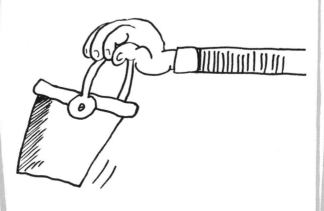

Knock, knock...

Who's there?

Cattle.

Cattle who?

Cattle get out if you open
the door, I'll come in through
the window!

Knock, knock...

Who's there?

Phillipa.

Phillipa who?

Phillipa bath, I'm really dirty.

Knock, knock...

Who's there?

Ivor.

Ivor who?

Ivor got my fingers stuck
in your letter box!

Knock, knock...

Who's there?

Brewster.

Brewster who?

Brewster wakes me up
every morning singing
cock-a-doodle do!

Knock, knock...

Who's there?

Marquis

Marquis who?

Marquis just snapped in the lock!

Knock, knock...

Who's there?

Doris

Doris who?

Doris closed - that's why
I'm having to knock!

Knock, knock...

Who's there?

Europe

Europe who?

Europe bright and early today!

Knock, knock...

Who's there?

Fantasy.

Fantasy who?

Fantasy walk in the park?

Knock, knock...

Who's there?

Leslie.

Leslie who?

Leslie town before they catch us!

Knock, knock...

Who's there?

Wade.

Wade who?

Wade up little Susie!

Knock, knock...

Who's there?

Carib.

Carib who?

Was it the antlers
that gave it away?

Knock, knock...

Who's there?

Wayne.

Wayne who?

Wayne, Wayne go away,
come again another day!

Knock, knock...

Who's there?

Andy.

Andy who?

Andy man!

Knock, knock...

Who's there?

April.

April who?

April will make you feel better!

Knock, knock...

Who's there?

Robin.

Robin who?

Robin the piggy bank again!

Knock, knock...

Who's there?

Emma.

Emma who?

Emma not going to tell you again!

Knock, knock...

Who's there?

Element.

Element who?

Element to tell you she
can't come today!

Knock, knock...

Who's there?

Arthur.

Arthur who?

Arthur gotten again!

Knock, knock...

Who's there?

Ivor.

Ivor who?

**Ivor message
for a Mr Smith!**

Knock, knock...

Who's there?

Shirley.

Shirley who?

Shirley you know the sound
of my voice by now?

Knock, knock...

Who's there?

Jester.

Jester who?

Jester minute I've forgotten!

Knock, knock...

Who's there?

Nipper

Nipper who?

Nipper round the back and
pass me my sunglasses!

Knock, knock...

Who's there?

Franz.

Franz who?

Franz, Romans, countrymen,
lend me your ears!

Knock, knock...

Who's there?

Zinka.

Zinka who?

Zinka da ship!

Knock, knock...

Who's there?

A little old lady.

A little old lady who?

I didn't know
you could yodel!

Knock, knock...

Who's there?

Bud.

Bud who?

Bud, sweat and tears!

Knock, knock...

Who's there?

Quacker.

Quacker who?

Quacker another bad joke
and I'm leaving!

Knock, knock...

Who's there?

Morse

Morse who?

Morse come in as quickly
as possible!

Knock, knock...

Who's there?

Postman Pat.

Have you got a parcel?

No, but I've got a black
and white cat!

Knock, knock...

Who's there?

Isabell.

Isabell who?

Isabell not working!

Knock, knock...

Who's there?

Oscar

Oscar who?

Oscar a silly question...

Knock, knock...

Who's there?

Tamara

Tamara who?

Tamara's my birthday, don't forget!

Knock, knock...

Who's there?

Cash

Cash who?

No thanks, but
I'll have some peanuts!

Knock, knock...

Who's there?

Cows go

Cows go who?

No, cows go moo!

Knock, knock...

Who's there?

Mandy

Mandy who?

Mandy lifeboats!

Knock, knock...

Who's there?

A guest

A guest who?

A guest you wouldn't recognise my voice!

Knock, knock...

Who's there?

Alpaca.

Alpaca who?

Alpaca suitcase and leave you
if you don't give me my own key!

Knock, knock...

Who's there?

Iona.

Iona who?

Iona have eyes for you!